W9-BUE-687

DREAMS AND
DEMANDS

Dan B. Allender
and Tremper Longman III

6 STUDIES FOR INDIVIDUALS, COUPLES OR GROUPS

ivp

InterVarsity Press
Downers Grove, Illinois

InterVarsity Press
P.O. Box 1400, Downers Grove, IL 60515-1426
World Wide Web: www.ivpress.com
E-mail: mail@ivpress.com

InterVarsity Press® is the book-publishing division of InterVarsity Christian Fellowship/USA®, a student
movement active on campus at hundreds of universities, colleges and schools of nursing in the United States
of America, and a member movement of the International Fellowship of Evangelical Students. For
information about local and regional activities, write Public Relations Dept., InterVarsity Christian
Fellowship/USA, 6400 Schroeder Rd., P.O. Box 7895, Madison, WI 53707-7895, or visit the IVCF website
at <www.intervarsity.org>.

Unless otherwise indicated, all Scripture quotations are taken from the Holy Bible, New Living Translation,
copyright ©1996, 2004. Used by permission of Tyndale House Publishers, Inc., Wheaton, Illinois 60189. All
rights reserved.

Design: Cindy Kiple

Images: Daly & Newton/Getty Images

ISBN 0-8308-2133-3

Printed in the United States of America ∞

P	18	17	16	15	14	13	12	11	10	9	8	7	6	5	4	3	2	1
Y	18	17	16	15	14	13	12	11	10	09	08	07	06	05				

CONTENTS

WELCOME TO
INTIMATE MARRIAGE
BIBLE STUDIES

DREAMS AND DEMANDS

When we look forward to marriage or actually get married, we do so with an idea, a hope, of what the future will bring. These wedding dreams are rarely clouded with the reality of issues to come. As obstacles come to the fulfillment of our dreams, often they turn to demands. This study explores some of these dreams and demands (children, money, jealousy, boredom, abuse) and offers both hope and help.

TAKING MARRIAGE SERIOUSLY

Most of us want to have a good marriage. Those who don't have a good relationship yearn for a better one, and those who have a good one want even more intimacy.

We want to know our spouse and be known by them. We want to be loved and to love. In short, we want the type of marriage desired by God from the beginning when he created the institution of marriage and defined it as involving leaving parents, weaving a life of intimacy together and cleaving in sexual bliss.

These studies delve into the wisdom of the Bible in order to learn what it takes to have not just a "good" marriage but one that enjoys the relational richness that God intended for a hus-

band and a wife. This divinely instituted type of marriage is one
that will

- Bring a husband and wife closer together
- Understand that marriage is one's primary loyalty to other human beings
- Be characterized by a growing love and knowledge of one another
- Be an arena of spiritual growth
- Allow for the healthy exposure of sin through the offer of forgiveness
- Be a crucible for showing grace
- Reflect God's love for his people
- Enjoy God's gift of sexual intimacy
- Share life's joys and troubles
- Have a part in transforming us from sinners to saints
- Bring out each other's glory as divine image bearers

And so much more! The Bible provides a wealth of insight, and
these studies hope to tap its riches and bring them to bear on our
marriage relationships.

USING THE STUDIES

These studies can be used in a variety of contexts—individual devotional life, by a couple together or by a small group—or in a
combination of these settings. Each study includes the following
components.

Open. Several quotes at the beginning give a sense of what married people say about the topic at hand. These are followed by a question that can be used for discussion. If you are using the DVD, you may want to skip this and go straight to the opening clip.

DVD Reflection. For each session we have an opening thought from Dan Allender, at times accompanied by an excerpt from our interviews with married couples, to get you thinking about the topic at hand. This material will provide fresh and engaging openers for a small group as well as interesting discussion points for couples studying together. You will find a question here to discuss after you watch the DVD clip.

Study. One or more key Bible texts are included in the guide for convenience. We have chosen the New Living Translation, but you may use any version of Scripture you like. The questions in this section will take you through the key aspects of the passage and help you apply them to your marriage. Sprinkled throughout the study, you will also find commentary to enrich your experience.

For the Couple. Here's an opportunity to make an application and commitment, which is specific to your marriage.

Bonus. These are further ideas for study on your own. Or if you are studying with a group, take time to do the bonus item with your spouse during the week.

We hope that these studies enrich your marriage. We encourage you to be brutally honest with yourself and tactfully honest with your spouse. If you are willing to be honest with yourself and with the Scripture, then God will do great things for your marriage. That is our prayer.

1

FRUITFUL OR BARREN?

"Don't get me wrong. I love our children. But we spend all our time and energy on them. We have no time for ourselves!"

"I'm scared. We have been trying to have children for some time now. I am afraid we won't be able to have them."

"My husband gets mad at me because I don't pay enough attention to him. But he's an adult; he can take care of himself. The children, on the other hand, absolutely need my attention."

▶ OPEN

Marriage involves two people, a husband and wife. But most couples have children, and children rightfully occupy a large part of their parents' attention. Children represent the hopes and dreams of their parents. When children are young, parenting involves a lot of physical energy. When they grow older, parents expend huge amounts of emotional energy. And even when they become adults and move away, it is hard to stop worrying about them. Children are a blessing to be sure, but they can also become occasions for significant relational damage to marriage. What are some issues that children bring to a marriage?

▶ DVD REFLECTION

What are some of the stresses that pregnancy brings to a marriage?

▶ STUDY

The story of Jacob and Rachel can shed some light on the complexity children bring to a marriage.

We readily understand the pain of a barren womb. If a couple can't have a baby, it can be devastating. However, in the ancient Israelite world the difficulty of barrenness was even greater. If a couple had no child, who would carry on the family name and occupy the family land? Further, in an age when there were no nursing homes, an aging couple without children had few avenues of support. And if the husband of a childless woman would die, she would be in dire straits. Husbandless and childless, she would have no standing in society. To understand Rachel's concerns, we need to keep in mind the horror of barrenness in her world.

Read Genesis 30:1-8.

When Rachel saw that she wasn't having any children for Jacob, she became jealous of her sister. She pleaded with Jacob, "Give me children, or I'll die!"

²Then Jacob became furious with Rachel, "Am I God?" he asked. "He's the one who has kept you from having children!"

³Then Rachel told him, "Take my maid, Bilhah, and sleep with her. She will bear children for me, and through her I can have a family, too." ⁴So Rachel gave her servant, Bilhah, to Jacob as a

wife, and he slept with her. ⁵Bilhah became pregnant and presented him with a son. ⁶Rachel named him Dan, for she said, "God has vindicated me! He has heard my request and given me a son." ⁷Then Bilhah became pregnant again and gave Jacob a second son. ⁸Rachel named him Naphtali, for she said, "I have struggled hard with my sister, and I'm winning."

1. How do you relate to Jacob or Rachel in this story?

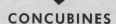

CONCUBINES

From the Bible and from other ancient Near Eastern texts of the time period, it is well known that some men took on secondary wives, also known as concubines. As in Genesis 30, the reason often had to do with the barrenness of the primary wife, in this case Rachel.

Though it was practiced in the ancient Near East, was it something that God desired? From the text that establishes marriage, Genesis 2:23-25, we are confident that God instituted a monogamous form of marriage: that is, one husband has one wife. However, the Old Testament law does not condemn the practice of having multiple wives but regulates it by providing support to the least loved of the wives (Exodus 21:7-11).

Though the practice is not condemned, the Old Testament clearly teaches that God did not want the men among his people to take multiple wives and concubines. Whenever a biblical character has more than one wife, the resultant problems are tremendous.

2. What makes Rachel's demand in verse 1 wrong?

3. What makes Jacob's response inappropriate (v. 2)?

4. How could Jacob have confronted what was wrong in what Rachel was saying without denying her legitimate desire?

5. Is it possible to have children but be barren? Explain.

6. How can a marriage suffer when the focus is on children?

7. What are some ways spouses tend to manipulate each other?

▼

LONELINESS, LINEAGE AND SECURITY

In response to Adam and Eve's sin, God punishes them with a curse (Genesis 3:16-19). The focus of their respective curses reveals something about the nature of men and women. Adam's work is affected by the curse; it will be permeated by futility. Eve's curse is in the area of relationship, with the result that she will be lonely. Both of their lives will now end in death. In the light of this, we can see the significance of children and why parents have their attention drawn to their children, sometimes obsessively. A woman may feel that children are the answer to her loneliness. To a man, children may represent help in a difficult world. To both of them, children represent a lineage, a mode of survival in the memory of their descendants beyond their death.

8. What two or three things would you say to Jacob and Rachel?

▶ FOR THE COUPLE

What do you need to confess to each other about how you have manipulated each other?

For the couple without children: Discuss the future and your plans to have children or not. Commit yourselves to spend regular time alone with each other even after having children.

For the couple with children: How well have you maintained your relationship since having children?

Have you periodically had times away from the children to be alone together? Why or why not?

Discuss ideas for how to set aside time alone.

▶ BONUS

Genesis 29 tells how Jacob was tricked into marrying Leah and then worked seven years to also marry Rachel. Read Genesis 30:9-21 and describe how the relationship evolves between Rachel and Leah. Name the nature of Rachel's fears. What does this tell you about what happens when desires turn into demands?

MANDRAKES IN GENESIS 30:9-21

Mandrakes were used as an aphrodisiac in the ancient world. In the story, sex is work with the hope of producing children. In their competition to outdo each other in childbearing, Leah and Rachel have been keeping Jacob busy. It may have been that he needed the help. But the presence of the mandrakes probably indicates that Jacob has become little more than a baby-making tool.

2

FOR RICHER
OR FOR POORER

"We have plenty of money. But we work all the time. We never see each other. Makes me wonder what we're working so hard for."

"He's lazy. I need to be home to raise the kids, but he is constantly being fired because he doesn't give any effort to his job."

"It's not like I want a new Mercedes or anything like that, just something presentable so I'm not embarrassed when I drive to work."

"Money, money, money—is that all you ever think about?"

"I just saw the credit card bill. How do you expect me to pay that?"

▶ OPEN

For richer or for poorer . . . When something is singled out for mention in traditional wedding vows, that's a sure signal that it is an area that requires special vigilance in a marriage. Money is necessary. In our society, without money we are in the streets begging for food. Everyone needs to be concerned about money to survive. Do you think it is important that couples talk about money? Why or why not?

▶ DVD REFLECTION

How have you been able to resolve a conflict over money in your marriage?

▶ STUDY

Every young couple enters marriage with different backgrounds and expectations. Even if they come from the same economic stratum, their parents may have had different attitudes toward money and different spending and saving patterns. And older couples with large incomes and savings may still fight over how to invest and spend their money. The struggle over finances never really ends. Proverbs offers us some guidance in how to think about money.

Read Proverbs 30:5-9.

⁵Every word of God proves true.
    He is a shield to all who come to him for protection.
⁶Do not add to his words,
    or he may rebuke you and expose you as a liar.
⁷O God, I beg two favors from you;
    let me have them before I die.
⁸First, help me never to tell a lie.
    Second, give me neither poverty nor riches!
    Give me just enough to satisfy my needs.
⁹For if I grow rich, I may deny you and say, "Who is the LORD?"
    And if I am too poor, I may steal and thus insult God's
        holy name.

1. What are the dangers of being poor?

2. What are the dangers of being rich?

3. Though a happy medium is advocated by the proverb, can you think of dangers of being middle-class?

PROVERBS ON MONEY

In focusing on just one proverb in Proverbs, we run the risk of distorting the message of the book. After all, the proverb as a literary form does not pretend to give a well-rounded discussion of a topic. It is a provocative statement that gets one thinking; it is true if applied in the right situation. Proverbs includes a number of individual statements about money, and the whole book deserves careful study. That the book is not against money in principle may be seen in a passage like 3:9-10, where wealth is the reward of someone who worships the Lord. Nonetheless, the book also notes that even fools sometimes get wealthy (11:18), though such wealth will not last. In the final analysis, wisdom and godliness are much more important than money (15:16). Proverbs 30:5-9, though just one proverb, gives a married couple a lot to consider concerning their attitude toward money.

Read Matthew 6:19-34.

[19]"Don't store up treasures here on earth, where moths eat them and rust destroys them, and where thieves break in and steal. [20]Store your treasures in heaven, where moths and rust cannot destroy, and thieves do not break in and steal. [21]Wherever your treasure is, there the desires of your heart will also be.

[22]"Your eye is a lamp that provides light for your body. When your eye is good, your whole body is filled with light. [23]But when your eye is bad, your whole body is filled with darkness. And if the light you think you have is actually darkness, how deep that darkness is!

[24]"No one can serve two masters. For you will be devoted to one and despise the other. You cannot serve both God and money.

[25]"That is why I tell you not to worry about everyday life—whether you have enough food and drink, or enough clothes to wear. Isn't life more than food, and your body more than clothing? [26]Look at the birds. They don't plant or harvest or store food in barns, for your heavenly Father feeds them. And aren't you far more valuable to him than they are? [27]Can all your worries add a single moment to your life?

[28]"And why worry about your clothing? Look at the lilies of the field and how they grow. They don't work or make their clothing, [29]yet Solomon in all his glory was not dressed as beautifully as they are. [30]And if God cares so wonderfully for wildflowers that are here today and thrown into the fire tomorrow, he will certainly care for you. Why do you have so little faith?

[31]"So don't worry about these things, saying 'What will we eat?

What will we drink? What will we wear?' ³²These things dominate the thoughts of unbelievers, but your heavenly Father already knows all your needs. ³³Seek the Kingdom of God above all else, and live righteously, and he will give you everything you need.

³⁴"So don't worry about tomorrow, for tomorrow will bring its own worries. Today's trouble is enough for today."

4. How realistic do you find Jesus' words on money? Explain.

▼

CONTEXT: THE SERMON ON THE MOUNT

Jesus' ministry patterns the redemptive acts of the Old Testament in order to make an important theological point. The text for this study comes from the Sermon on the Mount. Matthew sets this sermon not long after the wilderness temptations (Matthew 3:1-11). The forty days in the wilderness reflect the forty years Israel spent in the wilderness before entering the Promised Land. Jesus, though, shows that he is the obedient Son of God, since he does not give in to temptation as Israel did.

The fact that Jesus gives this sermon on a mountain is to remind us of Mount Sinai in the Old Testament. Jesus is talking about the law in the sermon, and God delivered the law to Moses on Mount Sinai. Jesus is the divine lawgiver. We are to hear his words as the words of God himself.

5. This text tells us that God will take care of his children according to their needs. Have you found this to be true from your experience?

6. How does one "store up treasures in heaven"?

7. Is it always wrong to make more money than you need? Why or why not?

8. Is it always wrong to make decisions based on money? Why or why not?

9. If a couple worries a lot about money, what does that probably indicate?

10. A husband and a wife will frequently enter a marriage with different histories and styles of working, saving, investing, spending and giving away money, and these differences easily escalate into significant conflict. How can this be avoided or dealt with?

▶ FOR THE COUPLE

Take a moment to assess your money situation. Would you consider yourself rich? poor? getting by?

Are you contented with your present financial situation, or do you find it an occasion for anxiety or even panic?

In what ways do you bring your financial situation to Christ?

In what ways do you tend to keep your finances separate from your spiritual life?

CONTEXT: ECCLESIASTES

The book of Ecclesiastes is difficult to understand on first reading. What is a book that keeps saying life is meaningless doing in the Bible? A close reading shows that the bulk of the book represents the teaching a wise man, who goes by the title "Teacher," as he reflects on life "under the sun," that is, apart from the illuminating truth of God. Another speaker at the end uses the Teacher's words to warn his son about the dangers of staying "under the sun." The Teacher certainly is insightful about life in a fallen world, and when he talks about money, we should listen to what he says.

▶ BONUS

Read Ecclesiastes 5:10-11. Why is it that those who love money never have enough?

How does a person know if they love money?

Reflect on how much you think about money and how much you talk about it. How important is money to your decision-making?

3

JEALOUSY: THE PASSION TO PROTECT—OR DESTROY

"I'm worried that my wife is spending too much time with my friend Rich. They work out together and have lunch frequently. But I know that I should just trust the Lord, since jealousy is always wrong."

"I can't stand to think of him spending any time with any woman anywhere. If I could I would keep him in my sights all the time. He's never been unfaithful, but I want to make sure he never is."

▶ OPEN

Marriage is an exclusive commitment between one man and one woman. It is a special, unique relationship. Unlike friendship or even other family relationships (parent-child, sibling-sibling), marriage allows one and only one spouse. This intimacy is expressed in many ways, including through sexual intercourse, an act reserved for marriage.

However, in our culture it is not possible or right to cut off all relationships with people of the other sex. Most men and women have friends and colleagues of the other sex. Jealousy is a real possibility in such a setting. Is it always wrong? How can we tell?

▶ DVD REFLECTION

How can jealousy be properly expressed?

▶ STUDY

Read Song of Songs 8:6-7.

6Place me like a seal over your heart,
   like a seal on your arm.
For love is as strong as death,
   its jealousy as enduring as the grave.
Love flashes like fire,
   the brightest kind of flame.
7Many waters cannot quench love,
   nor can rivers drown it.
If a man tried to buy love
   with all his wealth,
   his offer would be utterly scorned.

Read 1 Corinthians 13:4-6.

4Love is patient and kind. Love is not jealous or boastful or proud 5or rude. It does not demand its own way. It is not irritable, and it keeps no record of being wronged. 6It does not rejoice about injustice but rejoices whenever the truth wins out. Love never gives up, never loses faith, is always hopeful, and endures through every circumstance.

ANCIENT SEALS

The woman asks the man to place her like a seal over his heart and on his arm. To understand her passion, we need to consider the appearance and function of seals in the ancient Near East. Archaeologists have uncovered hundreds, even thousands of seals from Israel and elsewhere, most especially ancient Mesopotamia (today Iraq).

There were two types. The stamp seal, as the name suggests, makes an impression on soft clay when pressed down on it. The cylinder seal is round and makes an impression when it is rolled across soft clay. Both are forms of identification: the symbol and name on each seal would be unique to the owner. The soft clay would be a clay tablet, perhaps a letter or a pot, and the impression demonstrates and claims ownership.

Seals were often worn around the neck on a string or pinned to the end of a sleeve. The woman is thus asking the man to claim and announce the fact that she owns him. He is hers and hers alone. She wants her personal mark of identification placed on his heart (representing his inner life) and his arm (representing his actions in the world). She wants to possess him utterly.

1. By using the image of the seal, the woman expresses her desire that the man own her. She wants him to possess her. How do you react to such a statement?

Should *possession* characterize a marriage relationship? Explain your response.

▼

DEATH . . . GRAVE . . .WATERS

Love is seen as even more powerful than death, the grave and waters. Modern readers can certainly understand that these comparisons assert the overwhelming power of love; this awareness is intensified when we realize that the poet is invoking ancient Near Eastern mythological ideas to make the point. The waters are the waters of chaos; in the ancient Near East they represented disorder. Death and the grave, both personified here, relate to the false gods of the Canaanites; Mot (Death) was the actual name of a god. Love is more powerful than even these powerful forces.

2. Is it only the woman who should commit herself in such a way to the man? Explain how you see the concept of marital "ownership" working.

3. What might be lost if a person self-surrendered to his or her spouse in the way the woman does in the Song?

What might be gained?

4. How would you define jealousy?

5. The Song of Songs speaks positively about jealousy. What value can jealousy have in a marriage?

CONTEXT: 1 CORINTHIANS 13

Paul's powerful statement about love is often treated as a free-standing piece of writing, but it has its place in the letter to the Corinthians as a whole. It is important to keep in mind that the preeminent problem Paul sees with the Corinthian church is divisiveness. Everyone claims to have a corner on the truth; even spiritual gifts are being used as weapons to claim superiority over others. It is in this context of community conflict that Paul talks about the nature and crucial importance of love.

6. Paul says "love is not jealous." How does this square with what we have seen in the Song of Songs?

7. What does negative jealousy look like?

8. How should a spouse handle unfounded jealousy in light of 1 Corinthians 13?

▶ **FOR THE COUPLE**

Talk with each other about past and present worries concerning faithfulness. Invite each other to be open and honest, thus constructing an attitude of confidence and trust in your relationship. If there is ungrounded suspicion or an unnecessary energy to control the other, be honest about that and see how you can assure each other that nothing actually threatens the relationship.

ORDEALS IN THE ANCIENT NEAR EAST

Numbers 5 is a surprising text, unique in the Old Testament. However, we have a lot of information about similar rituals from places like ancient Babylon and Assyria. It fits in with rituals that today we call "ordeals." The most typical ordeal in the ancient Near East was the river ordeal. If someone was suspected of a crime, they would be taken to the river and thrown in. If they were innocent they survived; if they were guilty they drowned. Many an innocent person probably died this way in ancient Mesopotamia, but Numbers 5 asserts that God was in control of the consequences of this drink ordeal.

▶ BONUS

Read Nahum 1:2-6. In what way is God jealous? What does this tell us about jealousy?

Read Numbers 5:11-31. What does this tell you about jealousy?

Are there any implications for today?

FEELING NO CONNECTION

"I think I love her, but I feel no real connection with her. To be honest, I'm bored."

"The thrill is gone."

"We have a contented, ordered life and relationship. I'm happy for a peaceful relationship. Before there were heights of passion but also depths of despair."

▶ OPEN

It is often said that the Bible is not about passion and romance but about commitment. While commitment *is* key, the mere presence of the Song of Songs in the Bible makes it clear that God desires passion in our marriages. To say that the Bible says nothing about romance is silly. But what happens when the embers of passion die down? Many couples subside into a life together without passion. Is commitment all we can hope for?

▶ DVD REFLECTION

Do you think what Dan Allender describes about getting through the times when there's no connection is realistic? Why or why not?

▶ STUDY

Read Ecclesiastes 1:8-10 (NRSV).

[8]All things are wearisome;
    more than one can express;
the eye is not satisfied with seeing,
    or the ear with hearing.
[9]What has been is what will be,
    and what has been done is what will be done;
    there is nothing new under the sun.
[10]Is there a thing of which it is said,
    "See, this is new"?
It has already been,
    in the ages before us.

Read Ecclesiastes 9:7-10 (NRSV).

[7]Go, eat your bread with enjoyment, and drink your wine with a merry heart; for God has long ago approved what you do. [8]Let your garments always be white; do not let oil be lacking on your head. [9]Enjoy life with the wife whom you love, all the days of your vain life that are given you under the sun, because that is your portion in life and in your toil at which you toil under the sun. [10]Whatever your hand finds to do, do with your might; for there is no work or thought or knowledge or wisdom in Sheol, to which you are going.

1. Ecclesiastes 1:8-10 says there is nothing new under the sun. Is this true?

Do you ever feel this way?

CONTEXT: ECCLESIASTES

Rule number one in interpreting any biblical book (or any book for that matter) is to read a passage in its context. This is particularly important yet somewhat difficult in Ecclesiastes because of its unique character. Ecclesiastes has two speakers. Most of the book contains the words of the Teacher, but the end of the book makes it clear that his words are quoted by another unnamed wisdom teacher who is using them as an object lesson to his son (see Ecclesiastes 12:8-14, in particular verse 12, which mentions the son).

The Teacher speaks as a person who has come to question his religious tradition because of what he experiences and observes. He looks for meaning but concludes that it is "meaningless" (see 1:2, 12:8 and many other places in his speech). After he tries to find meaning in work, money, pleasure, even wisdom itself, and fails, he advocates trying to enjoy whatever gusto one can get. After all, only death lies in the future. He makes this point in a series of carpe diem passages, including 9:7-10. In context, this passage should be read with a note of resignation.

2. What effect does boredom have on the enjoyment of life in general?

BOREDOM

It is noteworthy just how infrequently boredom is an issue in the Bible. Yet many people today complain of being bored. It may be that people in the ancient world did not have the luxury of boredom, which seems to be an issue in affluent societies. If one is concerned about finding food or surviving an invading army's siege, thoughts of boredom never arise. However, the book of Ecclesiastes reminds us that boredom was not completely absent from ancient Near Eastern cultures.

How about on marriage?

3. What are some unhealthy ways that people in our culture deal with boredom?

Does this help or hurt a relationship?

4. How convincing do you find the Teacher's advice to "live happily with the woman you love through all the meaningless days of life that God has given you under the sun. The wife

God gives you is your reward for all your earthly toil." (9:9)?

CONTEXT: SONG OF SONGS

The Song of Songs contains a number of love poems celebrating, and sometimes warning about, the love between a man and a woman. The intended readers are a married couple, and these songs encourage them to identify with the man and the woman as they express their love, both verbally and physically, toward each other.

5. Song of Songs says: "Kiss me again and again, for your love is sweeter than wine. How fragrant your cologne, and how pleasing your name! No wonder all the young women love you! Take me with you. Come, let's run! Bring me into your bedroom, O my king" (1:2-4). How does this passage from the Song of Songs contrast with the resignation of the Teacher in Ecclesiastes?

6. How can boredom develop in a marriage?

7. Is boredom an inevitable consequence of living with one person for a long time?

What can be done to bring passion back into a relationship?

▶ FOR THE COUPLE

Reflect together about your relationship. Have you let life bog you down in a routine? Strategize together about what you should do about it. Then independently plan something new that will be a pleasant surprise for your spouse.

▶ BONUS

What factors, other than boredom, can dampen the passion of a marriage? Discuss two or three, and ask how they can be avoided or fought in a marriage relationship.

In Acts 18:2-3, 18-19, 24-26; Romans 16:3-5; 1 Corinthians 16:19; and 2 Timothy 4:19, we read about a couple named Aquila and Priscilla. They are always mentioned together and many of these passages describe them as deeply engaged in furthering the gospel. Read these passages. Reflect on the benefits that a couple might receive from being engaged together in God's work, particularly the effects it might have on boredom and disconnection. What are the potential downsides?

5

WOUNDED HEART

"I find it difficult to be intimate because of the way I was treated as a child."

"Whenever we make love, I can't help but think of the time I was raped in college."

"I was never physically abused, but all my mother ever taught me about sex was that it was dirty. I know she was trying to keep me from getting pregnant before I got married, but I still can't shake the idea that what we're doing is gross."

"I think I treated sex too lightly before I got married. Now there is nothing really special about it."

▶ OPEN

Everyone enters marriage with a history, some more difficult than others. Leaving one's past to form a new union (Genesis 2:24) is easier to say than to do, especially if that past is traumatic. If a person grew up in a situation where trust was not fostered, then it is difficult to trust one's spouse immediately. What are some ways that the past can affect a marriage?

▶ DVD REFLECTION

What do you think of what Dan Allender said about how past abuse or hurts affect a marriage?

▶ STUDY

The story of Amnon and Tamar will help us consider how our past can affect our future and begin to talk about hope for healing beyond the pain.

Read 2 Samuel 13:1-22.

Now David's son Absalom had a beautiful sister named Tamar. And Amnon, her half brother, fell desperately in love with her. ²Amnon became so obsessed with Tamar that he became ill. She was a virgin, and Amnon thought he could never have her.

³But Amnon had a very crafty friend—his cousin Jonadab. He was the son of David's brother Shimea. ⁴One day Jonadab said to Amnon, "What's the trouble? Why should the son of a king look so dejected morning after morning?"

So Amnon told him, "I am in love with Tamar, my brother Absalom's sister."

⁵"Well," Jonadab said, "I'll tell you what to do. Go back to bed and pretend you are ill. When your father comes to see you, ask him to let Tamar come and prepare some food for you. Tell him you'll feel better if she prepares it as you watch and feeds you with her own hands."

⁶So Amnon lay down and pretended to be sick. And when the king came to see him, Amnon asked him, "Please let my sister

Tamar come and cook my favorite dish as I watch. Then I can eat it from her own hands." [7]So David agreed and sent Tamar to Amnon's house to prepare some food for him.

[8]When Tamar arrived at Amnon's house, she went to the place where he was lying down so he could watch her mix some dough. Then she baked his favorite dish for him. [9]But when she set the serving tray before him, he refused to eat. "Everyone get out of here," Amnon told his servants. So they all left.

[10]Then he said to Tamar, "Now bring the food into my bedroom and feed it to me here." So Tamar took his favorite dish to him. [11]But as she was feeding him, he grabbed her and demanded, "Come to bed with me, my darling sister."

[12]"No, my brother!" she cried. "Don't be foolish! Don't do this to me! Such wicked things aren't done in Israel. [13]Where could I go in my shame? And you would be called one of the greatest fools in Israel. Please, just speak to the king about it, and he will let you marry me."

[14]But Amnon wouldn't listen to her, and since he was stronger than she was, he raped her. [15]Then suddenly Amnon's love turned to hate, and he hated her even more than he had loved her. "Get out of here!" he snarled at her.

[16]"No, no!" Tamar cried. "Sending me away now is worse than what you've already done to me."

But Amnon wouldn't listen to her. [17]He shouted for his servant and demanded, "Throw this woman out, and lock the door behind her!"

[18]So the servant put her out and locked the door behind her. She was wearing a long, beautiful robe, as was the custom in

those days for the king's virgin daughters. [19]But now Tamar tore her robe and put ashes on her head. And then, with her face in her hands, she went away crying.

[20]Her brother Absalom saw her and asked, "Is it true that Amnon has been with you? Well, my sister, keep quiet for now, since he's your brother. Don't you worry about it." So Tamar lived as a desolate woman in her brother Absalom's house.

[21]When King David heard what had happened, he was very angry. [22]And though Absalom never spoke to Amnon about it, he hated Amnon deeply because of what he had done to his sister.

1. Why is Amnon "sick" because of his attraction to Tamar?

Is this the same as "lovesickness"? Why or why not?

How does the desire to do wrong come to be an urge that overpowers taboo, honor or even likely consequences?

2. What role does Jonadab play in the story?

CONTEXT: 2 SAMUEL 13:1-14

The story of Amnon and Tamar is narrated as part of the story of King David, who is father of both of them by different women. To understand the story's purpose in the larger plot, we must remember that David had been chosen by God to be the anointed king over Israel. He was chosen because of his heart, his devotion to Yahweh, as opposed to his predecessor, whom the people chose because he was taller than everyone else.

Early in David's reign, everything went well. He was faithful to God and established Jerusalem as the center of worship of Yahweh. God blessed him with victory and wealth. However, one day when he was supposed to be with the army, he saw the naked Bathsheba and slept with her. She conceived, and David tried to cover up his sin by calling her husband Uriah back from the front line, hoping he would sleep with her. When he didn't, David resorted to having Uriah killed on the front lines of battle. David thought he had successfully hidden his sin, but God knew and confronted him through the prophet Nathan. See also Psalm 51.

Though he repented and God forgave him, the rest of David's story is a sad one. His family essentially falls apart, with negative ramifications for Israel as a whole. The story of Tamar and Amnon is the first of several stories about the disintegration of David's family. In this connection we are to see how David's sin has horrible repercussions.

What does this tell us about the people from whom we seek advice?

3. What role does power play in the abuse?

AMNON'S CRIME

Amnon's crime is twofold. In the first place, he rapes Tamar. Second, they are related by blood through their father David, thus half-brother and half-sister, and such an incestuous pairing was not permitted under the law of Moses (see Leviticus 18:9, 11; 20:17; Deuteronomy 27:22). Tamar's plea that David would arrange their wedding if he did not rape her is best understood as a desperate attempt to forestall Amnon's aggression (see 2 Samuel 13:13). Amnon probably knows this, so her statement does not have the desired effect. And after he violates her, he throws her out, which compounds the evil.

4. What are the spiritual and psychological consequences of this sexual abuse?

5. Why do you think Amnon's "love" for Tamar turns to hate after he rapes her?

6. What long-term effects does this abuse have on those in the story?

AMNON, TAMAR AND ABSALOM

As it turns out, this episode essentially triggered the plot of the next seven chapters (through chapter 20). At the beginning of the story, it is likely that Amnon was next in line for the throne and Absalom right behind him. However, Amnon's sin against Absalom's sister engendered Absalom's intense hate. He did not act immediately but waited for the right time, two years later, to get his revenge: he had Amnon murdered at a party. These acts led to disaffection between Absalom and David and even a major civil war. In these chapters we can see the long-range disastrous consequences of Amnon's act of obsessive lust.

7. What are some other kinds of baggage that people bring to a marriage, and what effects does it have on the marriage?

8. What are some healing steps that can help us gain freedom from long-term baggage?

▶ FOR THE COUPLE

Sensitively discuss with each other patterns or events of past abuse and consider whether they may have an influence on your marriage today. If so, review the answer to question 8 and consider what healing steps might be appropriate.

▶ BONUS

Read 2 Samuel 11-12. Do you see any parallels between the story of David and Bathsheba and that of Amnon and Tamar?

Can you draw any conclusions from this?

6

IT TAKES A CHURCH...

"When Matt and I have a problem, we have no one we feel comfortable talking to about it."

"You know, after we had our baby, my wife experienced tremendous postpartum depression. I didn't know what to do, but our counselor was a great help."

"We have been in a married couples group at church for two years now. Of course we don't share everything, but it has been a real blessing to have people to talk to, especially those who have gone through things we are now going through."

▶ OPEN

Marriage unites two people so that they can face the chaos of life together. As Ecclesiastes puts it, "Two people can accomplish more than twice as much as one" (4:9). But all couples can find support from others who have experienced the same things they are going through. Ecclesiastes goes on to say, "Three are even better" (4:12). And there are times when couples cannot handle issues on their own. What are some ways that others have encouraged and supported your marriage?

▶ DVD REFLECTION

How is your marriage nurtured by your church, small group or Christian friends?

▶ STUDY

If it takes a village to raise a child, it takes a church—that is, other believers—to encourage the healthy growth of a marriage. Having considered some of the complexities of marriage, this study invites you to reflect on biblical passages that encourage the development of a support group, formal or informal, that can provide advice and help to a married couple, no matter what stage of marriage they are in.

Read the following selections from Proverbs.

Without wise leadership, a nation falls;
  there is safety in having many advisers. (11:14)

Fools think their own way is right,
  but the wise listen to others. (12:15)

The godly give good advice to their friends;
  the wicked lead them astray. (12:26)

Pride leads to conflict;
  those who take advice are wise. (13:10)

Get all the advice and instruction you can,
  so you will be wise the rest of your life. (19:20)

Plans go wrong for lack of advice;
  many advisers bring success. (15:22)

Plans succeed through good counsel;
>   don't go to war without wise advice. (20:18)

No human wisdom or understanding or plan,
>   can stand against the LORD. (21:30)

The wise are mightier than the strong, and those with
>   knowledge grow stronger and stronger.
So don't go to war without wise guidance;
>   victory depends on having many advisers. (24:5-6)

PROVERBS' ADVICE FOR MARRIED COUPLES

Proverbs is a book of advice. Its voice is that of a wise person, typically a father, who gives his son advice about how to live well. Included is counsel about how to avoid problems and, if a mistake is made, how to get out of trouble in the most dignified and efficient way.

Some of the Proverbs passages in this study have to do with running a nation, in particular waging warfare. However, the principles hold in other aspects of life, including marriage. A large portion of the advice that the father gives the son in Proverbs specifically concerns marriage (see especially Proverbs 5—7). So the whole book models the importance of getting wise counsel.

1. Proverbs 13:10 draws a contrast between those who are proud and those who take advice. Why does pride lead a person to ignore or reject advice?

Why would it be particularly problematic to let pride get in the way of seeking marital advice?

2. How can people combat a prideful attitude and open themselves up to instruction?

3. Are there times when advice should be rejected or ignored?

' How can you tell?

4. What distinguishes good advice from wicked advice (15:22)?

5. Do you think any marriage gets to the point that the spouses

no longer need the advice of others? Explain.

6. At what point do you think spouses should seek the help of a professional counselor?

7. Proverbs 21:30 seems to give the last word on advice and planning in general. What does it have to say to marriage partners?

▶ **FOR THE COUPLE**

Do you know people you can go for help in your marriage?

Do you think such people are necessary? If not, why not?

If so, and you have no such people in your life right now, where can you go to develop such relationships?

▶ **BONUS**

Brainstorm about the resources available in your church(es) and community that would be helpful for the support of marriages.

LEADER'S NOTES

My grace is sufficient for you.

2 CORINTHIANS 12:9 NIV

Leading a Bible discussion can be an enjoyable and rewarding experience. But it can also be *scary*—especially if you've never done it before. If this is your feeling, you're in good company. When God asked Moses to lead the Israelites out of Egypt, he replied, "O Lord, please send someone else to do it" (Ex 4:13 NIV). It was the same with Solomon, Jeremiah and Timothy, but God helped these people in spite of their weaknesses, and he will help you as well.

You don't need to be an expert on the Bible or a trained teacher to lead a Bible discussion. The idea behind these inductive studies is that the leader guides group members to discover for themselves what the Bible has to say. This method of learning will allow group members to remember much more of what is said than a lecture would.

These studies are designed to be led easily. As a matter of fact, the flow of questions through the passage from observation to interpretation to application is so natural that you may feel that the studies lead themselves. This study guide is also flexible. You can use it with a variety of groups—student, professional, neighborhood or church groups. Each study takes forty-five to sixty minutes in a group setting.

There are some important facts to know about group dynamics and encouraging discussion. The suggestions listed below should enable you to effectively and enjoyably fulfill your role as leader.

PREPARING FOR THE STUDY

1. Ask God to help you understand and apply the passage in your own life. Unless this happens, you will not be prepared to lead others. Pray too for the various members of the group. Ask God to open your hearts to the message of his Word and motivate you to action.

2. Read the introduction to the entire guide to get an overview of the entire book and the issues which will be explored.

3. As you begin each study, read and reread the assigned Bible passage to familiarize yourself with it.

4. This study guide is based on the New Living Translation of the Bible. It will help you and the group if you use this translation as the basis for your study and discussion.

5. Carefully work through each question in the study. Spend time in meditation and reflection as you consider how to respond.

6. Write your thoughts and responses in the space provided in the study guide. This will help you to express your understanding of the passage clearly.

7. It might help to have a Bible dictionary handy. Use it to look up any unfamiliar words, names or places. (For additional help on how to study a passage, see chapter five of *How to Lead a LifeGuide Bible Study,* InterVarsity Press.)

8. Consider how you can apply the Scripture to your life. Remember that the group will follow your lead in responding to the studies. They will not go any deeper than you do.

9. Once you have finished your own study of the passage, familiarize yourself with the leader's notes for the study you are leading. These are designed to help you in several ways. First, they tell you the purpose the study guide author had in mind when writing the study. Take time to think through how the study questions work together to accomplish that purpose. Second, the notes provide you with additional background information or suggestions on group dynamics for various questions. This informa-

tion can be useful when people have difficulty understanding or answering a question. Third, the leader's notes can alert you to potential problems you may encounter during the study.

10. If you wish to remind yourself of anything mentioned in the leader's notes, make a note to yourself below that question in the study.

LEADING THE STUDY

1. Begin the study on time. Open with prayer, asking God to help the group to understand and apply the passage.

2. Be sure that everyone in your group has a study guide. Encourage the group to prepare beforehand for each discussion by reading the introduction to the guide and by working through the questions in the study.

3. At the beginning of your first time together, explain that these studies are meant to be discussions, not lectures. Encourage the members of the group to participate. However, do not put pressure on those who may be hesitant to speak during the first few sessions. You may want to suggest the following guidelines to your group.

   • Stick to the topic being discussed.

   • Your responses should be based on the verses that are the focus of the discussion and not on outside authorities such as commentaries or speakers.

   • Anything said in the group is considered confidential and will not be discussed outside the group unless specific permission is given to do so.

   • Listen attentively to each other and provide time for each person present to talk.

   • Pray for each other.

4. Play the DVD clip from the *Intimate Marriage DVD* and use the DVD reflection question to kick off group discussion. You can move directly from there to the beginning of the study section. Or, if you wish, you can also have a group member read the introduction aloud and then you can discuss the question in the "Open" section. If you do not have the DVD, then

be sure to kick off the discussion with the question in the "Open" section.

The "Open" question and the DVD clip are meant to be used before the passage is read. They introduce the theme of the study and encourage members to begin to open up. Encourage as many members as possible to participate, and be ready to get the discussion going with your own response.

This section is designed to reveal where your thoughts or feelings need to be transformed by Scripture. That is why it is especially important not to read the passage before the discussion question is asked. The passage will tend to color the honest reactions people would otherwise give because they are, of course, supposed to think the way the Bible does.

5. Have a group member (or members if the passage is long) read aloud the passage to be studied. Then give people several minutes to read the passage again silently so that they can take it all in.

6. Question 1 will generally be an overview question designed to briefly survey the passage. Encourage the group to look at the whole passage, but try to avoid getting sidetracked by questions or issues that will be addressed later in the study.

7. As you ask the questions, keep in mind that they are designed to be used just as they are written. You may simply read them aloud. Or you may prefer to express them in your own words.

   There may be times when it is appropriate to deviate from the study guide. For example, a question may have already been answered. If so, move on to the next question. Or someone may raise an important question not covered in the guide. Take time to discuss it, but try to keep the group from going off on tangents.

8. The sidebars contain further background information on the texts in the study. If they are relevant to the course of your discussion, you may want to read them aloud. However, to keep the discussion moving, you may want to omit them and allow group members to read them on their own.

9. Avoid answering your own questions. If necessary, repeat or rephrase them until they are clearly understood. Or point out something you read in the

leader's notes to clarify the context or meaning. An eager group quickly becomes passive and silent if they think the leader will do most of the talking.

10. Don't be afraid of silence. People may need time to think about the question before formulating their answers.

11. Don't be content with just one answer. Ask, "What do the rest of you think?" or "Anything else?" until several people have given answers to the question.

12. Acknowledge all contributions. Try to be affirming whenever possible. Never reject an answer. If it is clearly off-base, ask, "Which verse led you to that conclusion?" or again, "What do the rest of you think?"

13. Don't expect every answer to be addressed to you, even though this will probably happen at first. As group members become more at ease, they will begin to truly interact with each other. This is one sign of healthy discussion.

14. Don't be afraid of controversy. It can be very stimulating. If you don't resolve an issue completely, don't be frustrated. Move on and keep it in mind for later. A subsequent study may solve the problem.

15. Periodically summarize what the group has said about the passage. This helps to draw together the various ideas mentioned and gives continuity to the study. But don't preach.

16. At the end of the Bible discussion, give couples an opportunity to discuss the "For the Couple" section and make the application personal. It's important to include this in your group time so that couples don't neglect discussing this material. Of course, sometimes couples may need to discuss the topic long beyond the five minutes of group time allotted, but you can help them get started in the meeting.

17. Encourage group members to work on the "Bonus" section between meetings as a couple or on their own. Give an opportunity during the session for people to talk about what they are learning.

18. End on time.

Many more suggestions and helps on leading a couples group are found in the *Intimate Marriage Leader's Guide.*

COMPONENTS OF SMALL GROUPS

A healthy small group should do more than study the Bible. There are four components to consider as you structure your time together.

Nurture. Small groups help us to grow in our knowledge and love of God. Bible study is the key to making this happen and is the foundation of your small group.

Community. Small groups are a great place to develop deep friendships with other Christians. Allow time for informal interaction before and after each study. Plan activities and games that will help you get to know each other. Spend time having fun together—going on a picnic or cooking dinner together.

Worship and prayer. Your study will be enhanced by spending time praising God together in prayer or song. Pray for each other's needs—and keep track of how God is answering prayer in your group. Ask God to help you to apply what you are learning in your study.

Outreach. Reaching out to others can be a practical way of applying what you are learning, and it will keep your group from becoming self-focused. Host a series of evangelistic discussions for your friends or neighbors. Clean up the yard of an elderly friend. Serve at a soup kitchen together, or spend a day working on a Habitat house.

Many more suggestions and helps in each of these areas are found in *Small Group Idea Book.* Information on building a small group can be found in *The Big Book on Small Groups* (both from InterVarsity Press). Reading through one of these books would be worth your time.

STUDY NOTES

Study 1. Fruitful or Barren? Genesis 30:1-8.

Purpose: To recognize the proper role children should play in a marriage relationship.

Question 1. This question asks for reaction, and people may answer in various ways. Some will feel sorry for Jacob; others will think he is weak-minded. Probably most will be turned off by Rachel, who seems frantic and demanding. If so, the leader may want to remind people of the dire circumstances in which a barren woman would find herself in ancient Israel.

Question 2. Demand for a child leads Rachel to undermine her husband throughout this account. She requires Jacob to give her something, children, beyond his control. She blames him and thus alienates him. She also forces a secondary wife on him. All this would estrange Jacob from his wife; as the story continues we will see that his taking the concubine brings all kinds of heartache into the midst of the family.

Question 3. He flies into a rage. This could only push Rachel further away. He seems to attack her because of his fear and lack of control.

Question 4. He could have found ways to reassure her. She is obviously frightened at the consequences of barrenness; if he had found ways to fill that void, it would have helped. He could also have shown that he recognized the legitimacy of her fear.

Question 5. Inhospitable ground that can't bear fruit is barren. Many a barren woman feels as if her womb, and by extension her whole self, is damaged goods. A mother or father who has children may not be able to provide good ground in which they can grow; that is, a parent can be psychologically and spiritually barren.

Question 6. Just as Rachel pours her energies into having a child to the detriment of her relationship with Jacob, so you can pour all your energies into a child to the detriment of the relationship with your spouse.

Question 7. We manipulate each other in a vast variety of ways. Here we see Rachel manipulating Jacob through fear and guilt. She angers Jacob by blaming him for her barrenness. She shames him into accepting a secondary wife. Nearly every marriage is plagued by a suspicion that other couples are happier.

Question 8. This question may elicit a number of different responses. Some may want to tell both Jacob and Rachel to trust the Lord and not try to manipulate the situation by finding ways to have children through the customs of the day. They may want to encourage them to find happiness in each other rather than through children. They may want to tell Rachel not to approach Jacob in such an aggressive way.

Bonus. When desires turn into demands, the consequences are usually bad. Here Rachel's desire for a child leads to the escalation of a competition between her and her sister Leah. This competition rends the family apart far into the future (see the consequences on the children by reading the account of Joseph and his brothers in Gen 37—50).

Study 2. For Richer or for Poorer. Proverbs 30:5-9; Matthew 6:19-34.

Purpose: To explore the affect money, or its lack, has on a marriage relationship.

Question 1. If one is poor, then one may be tempted to get money by illegitimate means. Or a poor person may be tempted to invest obsessive energy in figuring out how to get enough to stay alive and sheltered.

Question 2. Riches can lead to complacency. Rich persons can feel they do not need anyone else and may lose sight of their need for God (see Ps 30).

Question 3. The proverb suggests that someone who has enough and not too much can be contented without being complacent. Such a person will still need to exercise trust in the Lord rather than their bank account. And this is theoretically true. But many middle-class people think they have too little. They have a car, a house, food and much, much more. However, they want even more—a better car, a bigger house.

Questions 4-5. The discussion here will be free-flowing. Of course, since Jesus said it, most Christians will admit that what he says is true. But if there is honest discussion, people will probably question whether it really is possible to survive in our world without some anxious consideration and striving after money.

Question 6. With this language Jesus calls his disciples to put their efforts into matters that build up the kingdom of heaven here on earth rather than pursuing financial gain.

Questions 7-8. It is always wrong to pursue money for money's sake or to make decisions based only on how much money one will make. Jesus is talking about priority. People tend to make money-related decisions out of fear and the assumption that security comes through having a lot of money. Jesus is telling people to get their priorities straight. He is alleviating their fears by telling them that their heavenly Father can provide for them. Make decisions based on higher spiritual goals, he says, and God will take care of you.

Question 9. It most likely indicates that money is too important. It may even indicate that money and one's work have become an idol—something treated as more important than God himself. It is a signal that the couple should work at getting their priorities straight again.

Question 10. The first and most important point, missed by many, is simply to be open and honest in discussing these issues. Do not assume that your ideas and background are automatically right. Expect to learn from your spouse. You may find that certain idols are exposed that need to be dealt with.

Talk together about your goals. Strive to get your priorities right according to Jesus' Sermon on the Mount teachings. Are you storing your treasures in heaven or only on earth? Remember that a married couple may live harmoniously and agree perfectly about money, but be living an evil life (review the story of Ananias and Sapphira in Acts 5:1-11).

Some people argue on the basis of Ephesians 5 that the husband is the "head" and therefore the one and only legitimate decision maker about important matters. This is a faulty understanding of "head," which on analogy with Christ's relationship to the church means that the husband is to lay down his life for his wife. Most couples will best resolve money issues by talking together and trying to reach consensus. If consensus is not reached, then one or both are probably taking money matters too seriously.

Bonus. We are built to live in Eden, a place of tremendous abundance, but we live in a fallen world, and all the money in the world cannot satisfy us.

Study 3. Jealousy. Song of Songs 8:6-8; 1 Corinthians 13:4-6.

Purpose: To understand the constructive and destructive sides of jealousy in a marriage relationship.

Question 1. Some resistance might be anticipated, since women and men today feel uneasy about the idea of one person owning another. But is this because of our notions of individualism? Are we afraid to commit ourselves to another? Perhaps this would be a good opportunity to explore why people are hesitant to give themselves over to another person completely and unreservedly. Perhaps there have been past betrayals or simply a desire to retain control over one's life.

Question 2. In a marriage *both* partners should give themselves exclusively and totally to the other. In such a marriage the spouses strive toward the goal of mutual submission, where each looks out for the interests of the other (Eph 5:21-33; Phil 2:3-4).

Question 3. Of course to give oneself over to another in such a trusting way does open a person up to potential emotional harm. We are often afraid to give up control in this way. However, not to do so will keep a relationship very superficial. Avoiding any risk of betrayal will sacrifice intimacy.

Question 4. Some may define jealousy in a totally negative fashion as a destructive emotion, suspicious and controlling. A better understanding, especially considering the positive things the Bible says about certain forms of jealousy, is that jealousy is energy to protect a relationship that God intends to be exclusive. Jealousy has a positive as well as a destructive face.

Question 5. Jealousy first of all acknowledges that marriage is an exclusive relationship that brooks no rivals. If a husband or a wife suspects that their spouse may be threatening the boundaries of their relationship by cultivating an intimate association with another person, then there is nothing wrong and everything right about exerting constructive energy toward addressing the problem, beginning with expressing one's concern to the other. "You shouldn't be jealous" is not a legitimate response to such worries, since the Bible here and elsewhere acknowledges that jealousy is a positive thing in a marriage (when acted on appropriately; see following questions). Rather, the spouse should take great care to reassure his or her partner—and ensure—that nothing is going on that threatens the relationship.

Question 6. This word occurs in a context along with boastful, proud and rude, among other negative traits. So here Paul is talking about a different face of jealousy, a self-centered and controlling emotion rather than one that legitimately seeks to protect a relationship.

Question 7. It is ill-founded and destructive. It seeks to control out of fear and lack of trust rather than any legitimate concern about the thoughts or actions of the spouse. In its worse manifestations, it becomes physically and/or verbally abusive. Even when there is reason for suspicion, or even if suspicions are confirmed, healthy jealousy will *never* lead to inflicting physical harm.

Question 8. It would be counterproductive to get angry and defensive unless the jealousy is expressed in inappropriate ways. Reassure your spouse of your love and then be open about your relationship to help him or her come to understand that there is no reason to fear. Consider whether your spouse has a legitimate concern not about you, but about the person who he or she sees threatening the relationship. If so, then talk together about proper and improper behavior toward that person.

Bonus. *Nahum 1:2-6:* Our relationship with God is much like a marriage, at least viewed from our side of the relationship. That is, both are exclusive relationships: we can have only one spouse and only one God. If we do anything that threatens our relationship with a spouse, they have a legitimate reason to be jealous, and the same is true with God. Seeing God characterized by jealousy reminds us that jealousy is not an inherently evil or unhealthy emotion.

Nahum is a short book and unfamiliar to many readers. Nahum lived in the mid-seventh century B.C., while Assyria was still in existence and oppressing the people of God. The book is a prophecy and celebration of the coming destruction of Nineveh, the capital city of Assyria, an event that took place in 612 B.C. In this destruction the biblical prophets see the judging hand of God. Nahum 1:2-9 begins its prophetic anticipation of the fall of Nineveh with a psalm celebrating the jealous anger of God toward his enemies and continues in verses 9-15 by celebrating God's goodness toward his people.

Numbers 5:11-31: This passage describes an elaborate ritual for a suspicious husband. The ritual is strange to us, and it raises questions about the rights of a jealous wife, but it indicates again that jealousy is not an inherently wrong emotion. Its application for today might be that if feelings of jealousy are more than a couple can resolve themselves, they can seek help from a spiritually mature person, perhaps a pastor or a counselor.

Study 4. Feeling No Connection. Ecclesiastes 1:8-10; 9:7-10.

Purpose: To grapple with the devastating effects of boredom in a marriage relationship and consider ways to rekindle the passion.

Question 1. Certainly it often seems that there is nothing new on the world scene or in our own lives. Even though the sides shift, world history can be seen as one war after another. But on the other hand, the Bible elsewhere teaches God does indeed introduce new things into history (Num 16:30; Is 43:19). Remember (see "Context: Ecclesiastes") that the Teacher is a wise man who struggles with his theology.

Question 2. Boredom results from and intensifies a lack of engagement in life. If you are bored, you cannot muster the energy to enter life. If you are bored and disengaged from your marriage, it harms and even destroys this relationship that feeds on intimacy.

Question 3. People often try to remedy boredom in ways that only increase the problem. Some turn to alcohol or drugs or overeating. Others try to instill thrills in their life by an adulterous affair. Obviously dealing with boredom in these ways harms a relationship.

Question 4. The way he encourages his hearers to enjoy life with their wife seems to undermine the idea. After all, life is "vain" or meaningless (NIV). The way he speaks of it as a reward for one's toil makes it sound at best like a momentary respite in a bleak life.

This rather sad interpretation of these words is confirmed when we read the Teacher's other comments about wives and women in general elsewhere in the book (see especially 7:25-29).

Question 5. As is typical in Song of Songs, this short passage expresses deep desire for intimacy in relationship. The woman, who is speaking to and about her husband, quivers with anticipation of union.

Question 6. Boredom can occur when life together becomes overly predictable. It is easy to settle into a routine in which wife and husband are disengaged from each other, particularly when children are involved. Life becomes so busy that no thought or energy is given to the relationship.

Question 7. A couple will have to be intentional about thinking and planning together to engender passion and surprise. Each relationship is different, but couples should not get so bogged down in the "toil" of life that they forget how to play and surprise each other. Participants may have some good specific ideas to share with each other in this regard.

Study 5. Wounded Heart. 2 Samuel 13:1-22.

Purpose: To come to understand the effects of abuse on a marriage and to recognize the hope of redemption from that past.

General note. Abuse and its lasting effects on relationships are much larger than many imagine. Even if the object of serious abuse ourselves, we often don't realize how many of those around us are similarly traumatized. On the other hand, abuse takes place to different degrees. So even if someone wasn't severely traumatized, due to the nature of pervasive sin, we are all grappling with "issues" from the past.

Question 1. Amnon is sick with love because Tamar is a forbidden object of attraction to him: they are closely related by blood. The fact that she is denied him apparently makes his lust even stronger. In his case, his sickness shows an unhealthy obsession. However, it is not always wrong to feel such strong passion. The Song of Songs portrays the legitimate lovesickness of a woman for a man (Song 5:8).

In Amnon's case, once he was blinded by desire, there was nothing Tamar could do or say to prevent the abuse. This differs from the lovesickness pictured in Song of Songs 5:8: obsessive lust fails to see the other as cherished and worthy of honor, whereas true lovesickness gives honor and value to the other.

Question 2. Jonadab is described as shrewd, using a Hebrew word that elsewhere is translated "wise." Wisdom is skill in living. Jonadab, however, perverts his gift to come up with a strategy to rape Tamar, who is his cousin.

We should be very careful when we seek advice for solving our problems. We need to judge a person's character before allowing him or her to influence our thinking and decisions.

Question 3. Notice how Jonadab appeals to Amnon's power as the king's son (13:4) to encourage him to action. Then, of course, he uses that power to get Tamar alone and then his physical power to force her to have intercourse.

Question 4. Tamar names it as "shame." She will carry the shame of having been raped by her half-brother, and he will be considered a fool for doing it.

Question 5. The text does not tell us, so we must speculate a bit here. It may be that he now realizes that she is right: this act will destroy his reputation and probably invite the revenge of her brother Absalom. He may feel that she is to blame for the strong attraction he felt toward her. It is notable that Matthew 5:21-30 associates lust with anger. Lust entails a violent compulsion to be satisfied. In any case, the whole story shows just how self-centered Amnon is. He does not care about anyone, even someone he supposedly loves like Tamar.

Question 6. See the sidebar in the text.

Question 8. Healing can't come without confession. Confession is simply an acknowledgment of what is true without the effort to soften the harshness of reality. Confession not only names the failure of the log in our own eye; it also names the harm done to us by others. This naming requires we enter both what was done to harm and the vision of what was meant to be that was missed. To confess opens the heart to grief. A second major work of healing is to enter the sorrow associated with the harm we've done and has been done to us. To grieve loss also opens the heart to a righteous sense of anger for the losses incurred. Healng involves confession, grief and anger. This process also calls us to receive and to offer forgiveness. The healing path is not simple or finished fully in this life, yet the results of repentance is a series of freeing movements in our life that return us to the wonder of the cross. For further guidance see *The Wounded Heart* by Dan Allender (Colorado Springs: NavPress, 1995).

Bonus. While Scripture does not say that David forced Bathsheba to have sex, he did have relations with a woman who was forbidden to him, in this case because she was married. Abuse leads to abuse.

Study 6. It Takes a Church . . . Selections from Proverbs.

Purpose: To see that an individual or a couple don't have to be on their own as they struggle with issues of tensions and demands on their marriage

Question 1. Someone who is proud thinks they know everything and can do everything on their own. They don't need to listen to the advice of others because they do nothing wrong. Many people are so proud that they won't listen to any advice, but there are different degrees of pride.

It is particularly problematic to let pride get in the way of marital advice, because this will stifle the growth of the relationship. People who do not seek advice and correction of their mistakes are doomed to repeat those mistakes.

Pride on the part of one partner can be particularly difficult, especially if it means that the person isn't open to hearing criticism or advice even from their spouse.

Question 2. Pride arises from fear more than anything. We don't want to hear that we are mistaken or need others, because this means we aren't in total control of our life. The irony is that pride born of fear leads to a life of repeated mistakes. Proverbs teaches people not to fear other people or circumstances but to fear the Lord (1:7). If we fear the Lord, then we know their proper subordinate place in God's creation. We also know that we are not perfect. We need to acknowledge our weaknesses and failures, our need for other people and, most important, our need for God.

Question 3. Not everyone who offers advice is equally wise, and not everyone who is wise offers helpful advice every time they speak. The couple will have to judge advice prayerfully and in the light of the Word of God. It is important to seek more than one person's advice. If more than one wise person is saying the same thing, then that counsel should be given special attention (Prov 15:22).

Question 4. This question is best answered by reading the whole book of

Proverbs and seeing how wisdom, godliness and righteousness are described in contrast to folly, ungodliness and wickedness. Evil "leads astray" a person. In the ultimate sense, this means to move away from God and his will. As Proverbs often points out, evil advice leads to things that will squash life and promote death, while good advice does the opposite. Compare the picture of Woman Wisdom in Proverbs (8:1—9:6) with that of Woman Folly (9:13-18).

Question 5. No relationship is so deep or long-lived that it cannot be enhanced by the advice of others. Even the wise can grow in wisdom (Prov 1:5). If a person or couple thinks they have outgrown the need of advice, then they have fallen into the type of pride that can kill a relationship.

Question 6. While all relationships can benefit from the advice of others, some relationships have gotten to the point where the advice of an outside counselor is needed. Perhaps a conflict within the marriage has polarized the friends one normally goes to for advice. Perhaps these friends have run out of advice. Then there are certain needs that can benefit from experts' specialized understanding. The counselor might be an elder or pastor or a professional psychologist.

Question 7. The last word is God's. We can plan, and we can receive great advice, but God is sovereign over all. This should be encouraging, since we know that God loves and cares for us even more than our friends do. Where do we hear God's will for our lives most clearly? The Bible. This text should encourage us to hear the voice of our God through study of the Bible.